3 Flute Sonatas

To access audio visit:
www.halleonard.com/mylibrary

7275-9313-4876-5626

ISBN 978-1-59615-326-4

Music Minus One

EXCLUSIVELY DISTRIBUTED BY

HAL•LEONARD®

Visit Hal Leonard Online at
www.halleonard.com

Contact Us:
Hal Leonard
7777 West Bluemound Road
Milwaukee, WI 53213
Email: info@halleonard.com

In Europe contact:
Hal Leonard Europe Limited
Distribution Centre, Newmarket Road
Bury St Edmunds, Suffolk, IP33 3YB
Email: info@halleonardeurope.com

In Australia contact:
Hal Leonard Australia Pty. Ltd.
4 Lentara Court
Cheltenham, Victoria, 3192 Australia
Email: info@halleonard.com.au

Chamber Music

Chamber music may be roughly defined as music written for a small number of performers, each playing a separate and distinct part. The term (from the Italian *musica da camera*) was used by the Renaissance theorist, Nicola Vincentino, in his *L'Antico Ridotta Alla Moderna Prattica* (1555) to distinguish music of the kind heard in the chamber of a noble patron from that of church and folk music. Therefore, chamber music was primarily the exclusive social activity of the private salon, its original function being to provide musical enjoyment and camaraderie to its noble and royal participants who were, more often than not, remarkably skilled amateurs.

It remained the province of the private enthusiast until the beginning of the 19th century when several factors, including the decline of the nobility, the capabilities of the instruments, the aspirations of the players, and the growth of public concerts brought it out of the salon.

In any event, chamber music has always provided a sophisticated source of pleasure and enjoyment to both performer and listener and has challenged the greatest composers throughout musical history to produce their best creative efforts. Chamber music allows room only for essentials…the expression of particularly innermost ideas and the vehicle for intimate musical discourse and interaction. Its rich rewards do not depend upon virtuosic display, great splashes of color and sound, or sensational tonal and technical effects.

Baroque Chamber Music

Chamber music in the Baroque era (1600–1750) was the chief vehicle for the development of purely idiomatic instrumental writing, the most important forms being the trio sonata and the solo sonata. A direct outgrowth of the 17th century multi-sectioned canzona, the trio and solo sonatas inspired the first truly great writing for the violin which, according to many, was the undisputed instrument par excellence of the Baroque. Fast gaining in popularity towards the end of the century were the oboe and the transverse flute, both of which existed in much more pure and simple forms than their modern-day counterparts.

In the baroque sonata the structural interest lay in the texture of one or two treble parts highlighted against a bass line which, in its highest 18th century development, was often independent enough to enter into active dialogue and competition with the upper voices.

The practice of a clear supporting bass line governing the entire harmonic structure in any given ensemble composition was known as *basso continuo* or *thorough bass*. Often, a shorthand system of codified figures to indicate the harmonies was written under the bass line giving the performer the responsibility to "realize" and improvise upon the "figured bass." (Rare was the keyboard musician not proficiently versed in theory and practice to perform such a commonplace task at sight!) Realization could be accomplished on a number of chordal instruments, the more common being the organ for sacred music and the harpsichord for secular. Playing along with the continuo instrument to further emphasize the function of the bass line was any appropriate bass instrument such as bassoon, 'cello, or viola da gamba. Thus it was the combination of the two instruments, bass plus chordal, which made up the true baroque continuo.

A particularly pleasing and versatile combination is that of the viola da gamba and harpsichord: a blend of exquisite color and perfect balance.

Hardly anyone today is unacquainted with the harpsichord, the popular "plucked" keyboard instrument of the 17th and 18th centuries, but the viola da gamba, making its 20th century comeback somewhat later than the harpsichord, still remains unrecognized. Since Renaissance times, the incredible beauty of tone and expressive qualities of the viola da gamba have inspired composers to their finest efforts, assuring it a favorite place in both solo and chamber music literature.

The viola da gamba is the bass member of the viol family, and like its fellows, has six strings, a neck with movable frets and is bowed in an under-hand fashion. It is held between the knees like a cello and has no endpin.

The majority of chamber music in the 17th and 18th centuries was based on the basso continuo principle. This provided constant spontaneity and freshness to its performances as each keyboard player gave realizations governed by his own knowledge and personality and the interpretations of his companion players. Occasionally sonatas were written for a solo instrument and harpsichord obbligato, a fully composed part giving the keyboard equal partnership with the solo. Some of the greatest examples of this type come from J.S. Bach and include the Sonatas for flute and harpsichord and the Sonatas for viola da gamba and harpsichord.

Liner Notes by Jocelyn Chaparro

Contents

G.F. Handel: SONATA IN F MAJOR

Edited by Jean Antrim

Larghetto

3 taps precede music.

Ornamentation optional
Allegro

4 taps precede music.

4

Siciliana

6 taps precede music.

Allegro *

4 taps precede music.

*Staccato on repeat.

G. P. Telemann: Sonata in F Major

Vivace

Edited by Jean Antrim

4 taps precede music.

Largo

3 taps precede music.

Allegro

4 taps (2 measures) precede music.

8

B. marcello: SONATA IN F MAJOR
Op.2 No.1

Edited by Jean Antrim

Adagio

4 taps precede music.

Allegro

4 taps precede music.

piano

forte

9

piano

piano   *forte*

piano

Largo

3 taps precede music.

10

Allegro

4 taps precede music.

piano

The Rameau Trio

The Rameau Trio was founded in the early autumn of 1968 for the purpose of discovering and performing the finest works from the 17th and 18th century chamber music repertoire. The trio is especially dedicated to the performance of music by J.P. Rameau, in particular his rarely performed *"Pieces de Clavecin en Concerts,"* for which the trio has received enthusiastic acclaim from the musical world. The Rameau Trio has performed with brilliant success throughout the country. Based in the New York Metropolitan area, the trio maintains an active place in the higher echelon of the musical world. Contemporary works commissioned by the trio complete the group's repertoire.

Jean Autrim (flute) has had a varied musical career. As a scholarship student she has studied at Syracuse University and at the New School in New York City. Her private teachers include Murray Panitz, 1st chair with the Philadelphia Orchestra; Frances Blaisdell; and noted soloist and recitalist, Sam Baron. She has concertized extensively on the east coast as soloist and chamber musician, and has made numerous appearances with some of the leading symphony orchestras in the east. Of her performances in a recent Carnegie Recital Hall concert, Robert Jones of the *New York Times* said that she…"came through her ordeal of virtually non-stop flute playing beautifully; she sounded like one of the more promising flutists of the younger generation."
In addition to The Rameau Trio and other professional affiliations in the city, Miss Antrim maintains a teaching studio in New York and New Jersey.

Jocelyn Chaparro (harpsichord) has her graduate diploma from the Juillliard School of Music. She has studied with Albert Fuller, Anna Linde, Irene Bostwick, and Alfred Deller. Acclaimed as both a solo and chamber music performer, she has appeared extensively on both east and west coasts. At present she is professionally active as a free-lance harpsichordist in New York City and teaches at the United Nations International School. She also maintains a private studio for harpsichord and clavichord.

Mary Springfels (viola da gamba) is a native of Los Angeles. While attending U.C.L.A. as an English literature major, she developed an interest in early music, and performed with the John Biggs Consort and Roger Wagner Chorale. In 1968 she joined with New York Pro Musica Concert ensemble and has toured the U.S., Canada, and South America with them. She appears on the New York Pro Musica Decca recording of Shakespeare Theatre Music in the Golden Age. She has been cited as a "virtuosic talent with the treble and bass viol…a performer of great rhythmic vitality and skill."
Miss Springfels plays an 18th century viola da gamba whose maker's name has been lost during the various stages of restoration.